The Adventures of Tom Sawyer

by Mark Twain

Abridged and adapted by Lorri Ungaretti

Illustrated by James McConnell

A PACEMAKER CLASSIC

FEARON / JANUS / QUERCUS
Belmont, California

Simon & Schuster Education Group

Other Pacemaker Classics

The Adventures of Huckleberry Finn
A Christmas Carol
Crime and Punishment
The Deerslayer
Dr. Jekyll and Mr. Hyde
Ethan Frome
Frankenstein
Great Expectations
Jane Eyre
The Jungle Book
The Last of the Mohicans
Moby Dick
The Moonstone
The Red Badge of Courage
Robinson Crusoe
The Scarlet Letter
A Tale of Two Cities
The Three Musketeers
The Time Machine
Treasure Island
20,000 Leagues Under the Sea
Two Years Before the Mast
Wuthering Heights

ISBN 0–8224–9258–X
Library of Congress Catalog Card Number: 85–81087

Printed in the United States of America.

10 9 8 7 6
MA

Contents

1 Tom and Aunt Polly

"Tom!"

No answer.

"Tom!"

No answer.

"Where is that boy, I wonder? You TOM!"

No answer.

The old woman took off her glasses. She looked around the room. She spoke again. This time her voice was strong, but not very loud.

"Tom, if I get hold of you, I'll—"

She did not finish. By this time, she was bending down. She took the broom and pushed it around under the bed. The boy wasn't there. All she found under the bed was the cat.

"Where is that boy?"

She walked to the open door and looked out at the garden. No Tom. She shouted, "Y-o-u *Tom!*"

There was a noise behind her. She turned around just in time to see a small boy run out of the closet. She grabbed him by the shirt.

"There! I should've thought of the closet. What were you doing in there?" she said.

"Nothing," answered the boy.

"Nothing!" repeated the woman. "Look at your hands. And look at your mouth. What is all over you?"

"I don't know, Aunt Polly."

"Well, *I* know. It's jam—that's what it is. Forty times I've told you to leave the jam alone. I *told* you I'd hit you with the switch if you touched the jam again. Now hand me the switch."

She held the switch high in the air over the boy. Suddenly, the boy shouted, "Oh, my! Look behind you, Aunt!"

The old woman whirled around and snatched her skirt out of danger. The boy ran out the door. He jumped up and over the high board fence and was gone.

His Aunt Polly looked surprised for a moment. Then she laughed. "Hang that boy! Can't I learn

anything? Hasn't he played enough tricks on me? Well, I guess old fools are the biggest fools of all. But the boy never plays the same trick two times in a row. How am I to know what's coming? He seems to know just how much he can tease me before I get angry. And he knows just what to do to make me laugh when I am angry. I bet he will play hooky from school this afternoon. Then I'll have to make him work on Saturday. He hates work more than anything. But he's my own dead sister's boy, and I've got to bring him up right."

Tom did play hooky that afternoon. He went swimming and had a great time. While he was eating dinner, Aunt Polly started asking questions. She wanted to trap him into telling her that he had played hooky. She didn't know for sure, but she had a feeling that Tom had gone swimming.

"Tom, it was warm at school today, wasn't it?" she asked.

"Yes, Aunt Polly," answered Tom.

"Really warm, wasn't it?" she asked. Tom nodded. "Didn't you want to go swimming, Tom?"

Tom felt scared just then. Maybe Aunt Polly knew that he had gone swimming. He looked at her face. But he couldn't tell anything. "No, not very much," he answered.

His aunt reached out her hand. She touched Tom's shirt. "Well, you aren't too warm now," she said.

She felt proud of herself. She had touched Tom's shirt to find out if it was dry. She was sure that nobody knew why she had done that.

But Tom knew. He knew that he had to stop Aunt Polly from looking any further. "Some of us dumped water on our heads," he said. "My hair is still a little wet. See?" he said.

Aunt Polly was a little angry at herself. She had forgotten to check his hair. She thought of something else. "Tom, you didn't need to take off your shirt to dump water on your head, did you?" she asked. "So you didn't have to undo your shirt where I sewed it. Open your jacket, so I can see your shirt."

Tom stopped worrying. He opened his jacket. His shirt collar was sewed tight.

"Oh," said Aunt Polly. "I was sure you had played hooky from school. I thought you had gone swimming." She was glad that Tom had been good for a change.

Just then, Sid (Tom's half brother) said, "Didn't you sew his shirt with white thread? The thread on it is black now."

Aunt Polly's eyes opened wide. "Why, yes! I *did* use white thread! Tom!"

But Tom didn't wait to get in trouble. As he ran out of the door, he turned to Sid and said, "Sid, I'll get you for that."

2 Whitewashing the Fence

Saturday morning was bright and fresh. The sun was shining, and the trees were in bloom. Everything looked fresh and cheerful.

But Tom was not feeling very cheerful. He walked slowly out of the house. He was carrying a bucket of white paint and a brush with a long handle. He looked at the fence in front of the house. All gladness left him. Thirty yards of board fence nine feet high.

Tom sighed. He dipped the brush in the whitewash. He started painting the top part of the fence. Then he stopped. He looked at the one small streak he had painted. And he looked at the rest of the fence. Feeling gloomy, he sat down on a wooden box.

Just then, Jim came out of the gate. He was carrying a tin pail. The pail was used to collect water from the town pump. Tom had always hated the job of going to get water. But today, that job didn't seem so bad. "Say, Jim," Tom called. "I'll go get the water, if you'll do some whitewashing."

Jim shook his head. "I can't do that, Tom. Your aunt told me to go get the water. She said not to fool around with anybody. She said she thought you would ask me to whitewash. But I'm supposed to mind my own business and do my own job."

"Oh, never mind what she said," answered Tom. "That's the way she always talks. Give me the pail. I'll just be gone a minute. She won't ever know."

"Oh, I shouldn't," Jim said.

"I'll give you a white marble," Tom promised.

Jim began to look as if he might change his mind. "Besides, I'll also show you my sore toe," added Tom.

This was too much for Jim. He put down the pail, took the white marble, and leaned over to look at the toe. A moment later, Jim was flying down the street. He was carrying the pail in one hand and holding a hurting rear with the other. Tom was standing up, painting quickly. And Aunt Polly was walking away. She had a slipper in her hand and a satisfied look on her face.

Tom's energy did not last long after Aunt Polly left. He began to think of the fun he would miss that day. Soon his friends would be coming by. They would be planning adventures for the day. They would laugh at him for having to work.

Tom thought of giving things to his friends to get them to do some whitewashing. He took everything out of his pockets. He found marbles, parts of toys, and other junk. But he knew he didn't have enough to get out of painting. Suddenly, he had an idea.

Tom took up his brush and went to work. A few minutes later, Ben Rogers came down the street. He was hopping and skipping as he ate an apple. He made sounds like a steamboat. As he got closer to Tom, the sounds got louder and louder. Tom didn't pay attention to the steamboat. He just kept on whitewashing. Ben stopped. He stared at Tom for a minute. Then he said, "Hi, Tom! You're in a fix, aren't you?"

No answer. Tom stepped back and looked at his last paint stroke. He stared at it as if he were an artist. Then he gave his brush another sweep over the wood. Again, he looked at it carefully.

Ben walked up and stood beside Tom. Tom's mouth watered for Ben's apple. But he just kept on painting. Finally, Ben said, "Hello, Tom. You have to work, huh?"

Tom turned suddenly and said, "Oh, it's you, Ben. I didn't notice."

Ben began to tease Tom. "Say, I'm going swimming. Don't you wish you could? But you'd rather work, wouldn't you? Of course you would."

Tom stopped painting and looked at Ben for a moment. "What do you call work?" Tom asked.

"Well, isn't that work?" said Ben.

Tom started whitewashing again. Then he answered Ben in a calm voice. "Well, maybe it is work and maybe it isn't. All I know is that it suits Tom Sawyer."

"Oh, come on. You don't mean to say that you *like* it?" asked Ben.

The brush kept moving. "Like it?" Tom said. "Well, I don't see why I shouldn't like it. Does a boy get the chance to whitewash a fence every day?"

That put the job in a new light. Ben stopped eating his apple. Tom moved the brush back and forth. Then he stepped back to see how it looked. He added a touch here and there. Then he stepped back again and looked at it carefully.

Ben watched every move. He became more and more interested. Finally, he said, "Hey, Tom. Let me whitewash a little."

Tom thought about it. He was about to say yes.

But then he changed his mind. "No, I don't think you should, Ben," he answered. "Aunt Polly is pretty fussy about this fence. If it were the back fence, she wouldn't mind. But this one is right here on the street. It has to be done just right. I figure there's just one boy in a thousand that can do it the way it's got to be done. Maybe one boy in two thousand."

"Really?" said Ben. "Is that so? Oh, come on, Tom. Let me try. Just a little? I'd let you, if it was me."

Tom continued to paint. "Gee, Ben, I'd like to. But you know Aunt Polly. Jim wanted to do it, but she wouldn't let him. Sid wanted to do it, and she

wouldn't let Sid. Can you see my problem? If you were to start painting this fence, and anything happened to it—"

"Oh, shucks. I'll be careful," Ben promised. "Let me try. Say—I'll give you the core of my apple."

"Well, I don't know," Tom answered. "I don't think I should."

"I'll give you all of my apple!"

Tom gave up the brush. He had an unsure look on his face. But in his heart, he was happy. And the boy who had once been a steamboat started painting.

In the shade close by, Tom sat on a box. As he ate the apple, he made plans. He wanted other friends to help paint the fence. Boys came along all morning long. They came to tease, but they stayed to whitewash.

By the afternoon, the fence had three coats of paint on it. Tom had traded chances to whitewash for many treasures. He now had a kite, some string, a key that didn't open anything, a tin soldier, the handle of a knife, four pieces of orange peel, a brass doorknob, and lots of other things.

Tom had discovered something about people. He learned that the best way to make someone want something is to make the thing hard to get.

Tom stood up. He was pleased with himself. He walked into the house to report to Aunt Polly.

3 Tom Meets Becky

Aunt Polly was sitting in a room at the back of the house. She was knitting, and the cat was asleep on her lap. She thought that Tom had left his job long before. She wanted him to do the work. But she didn't really think he would finish it.

Tom walked up to his aunt. He said, "May I go and play now?"

Aunt Polly looked up. "How much have you done?" she asked.

Tom told her the work was finished. "Tom, don't lie to me," his aunt said.

She walked outside to look at the fence. She would have been happy if just a part of the fence had been painted.

But Aunt Polly was surprised. Not only was the fence painted, but it had three coats of paint on it!

"Well, I can't believe it," cried Aunt Polly. "There's no getting around it. You *can* work if you want to. Now, you can go and play." But first, she took Tom into the kitchen and gave him an apple. As soon as she turned her back, Tom took a doughnut, too.

Then he skipped out of the house and started walking through town. When he passed by the

Thatcher house, he saw a girl in the garden. She had yellow hair and blue eyes. She wore a white summer dress. Tom fell in love in a second. A certain Amy Lawrence was suddenly gone out of his heart. He had thought he would love Amy forever. But now he couldn't even think about her.

Tom stared at this new girl until she saw him. Then he pretended that he didn't know she was there. He began to show off by jumping and dancing around in different ways. He did his best handstands to get her attention.

The girl said nothing. She walked toward the front door. She stopped on the stairs. Tom sighed. He didn't want her to go away. But then his face lit up. Just before she went inside, the girl threw a flower over the fence to him.

Tom rushed over and picked up the flower. He put it inside his jacket, close to his heart or close to his stomach—he wasn't quite sure. He continued to show off in front of the house for a while. He hoped that the girl was near a window and could see him. But he didn't see her again that day.

Tom went home, in love and happy. He was in a good mood all through dinner. Aunt Polly wondered "what had got into the child."

Tom had a habit of stealing sugar from the sugar bowl. Most of the time he stole the sugar behind Aunt Polly's back. But, this time, he did it right in front of her. When she slapped his hand, he didn't seem to mind. He just said, "You don't hit Sid when he takes sugar."

Her answer was quick. "Well, Sid doesn't give me as much trouble as you do. Your hand would always be in the sugar if I weren't watching you."

A few minutes later, Aunt Polly went into the kitchen. Sid began laughing at Tom for getting caught taking sugar. Sid smiled as he reached for the sugar bowl. But then his finger slipped. The bowl dropped and broke.

Tom was full of joy. Finally, the "perfect boy" would get it! Tom decided not to say a word until his aunt came in. She would ask who had dropped the bowl. Then he would tell her and watch Sid get in trouble. He was so excited that he could hardly hold himself.

Aunt Polly came into the room. She was angry. "Now it's coming!" Tom said to himself.

But the next thing Tom knew, *he* had been hit. "Wait a minute!" Tom yelled. "What are you hitting *me* for? Sid broke it."

Aunt Polly stood still. She felt bad that she had hit the wrong boy. But she wasn't going to let Tom or Sid know that. "Well, I'll bet you deserved that slap, anyway," she told Tom. "I'm sure that you've been into some other mischief when I wasn't around."

Tom sat back. He felt sorry for himself. He thought about what would happen if he were

13

sick—maybe dying. His aunt would be bending over him. She would beg him for forgiveness. But he wouldn't forgive her. He would just turn his face to the wall. Then how would she feel?

Tom thought that maybe he would drown. People would carry his wet body home. And Aunt Polly would throw herself on him and cry. Then she would be sorry!

Tom got up and walked outside. He thought about the girl he had seen that day. Would she feel sorry for him? Would she cry and wish that she could hug him and make him feel better?

After it was dark, Tom walked past the Thatcher house. He saw a window with a lighted candle inside. "Is that her room?" he asked himself.

Tom was still thinking about how people would feel if he died. He lay down on the ground under the window. He lay on his back and took out the flower the girl had thrown to him. He crossed his hands on his chest, holding the flower. This was how he would look when he died. Maybe none of his friends would care. When this girl saw his body in the morning, would she care? Would she cry?

Just then, the window opened. Tom heard a servant's voice, just as someone threw a gallon of water out the window. Poor Tom was soaking wet. He jumped up and headed for home.

The next day, Tom met his love. He sat next to her at school. Her name was Becky Thatcher. Tom

put a peach on her desk, but she pushed it away. Tom put it back. She pushed it away again, but not as quickly. Tom returned it to its place. This time, she let it stay. He wrote her a note that said, *Please take it. I've got more.*

Tom and Becky talked awhile. Then Tom wrote another note. He hid it from Becky. She begged to see it. Tom said, "Do you promise not to tell anybody, as long as you live?"

Becky promised. Tom gave her the note. It said, *I love you.* "Oh, you bad thing!" Becky said. But she smiled and looked pleased.

The next day, Tom and Becky had lunch together. Everyone else had gone home for lunch, so they were alone in the classroom. They talked about things they liked and things they didn't like.

Then Tom said, "Say, Becky, have you ever been engaged to be married?" Becky shook her head.

"Well, would you like to be?"

"I guess so," Becky answered. "What is it like?"

"It isn't like anything else," Tom explained. "You tell a boy that you will never ever want any other boy. Then you kiss. That's all. Anybody can do it."

"Kiss?" asked Becky. "Why do you kiss? Does everybody do that?"

"Oh, yes," said Tom. "Everybody that is in love kisses. And remember what I wrote on that note to you? Well, we have to whisper that to each other, too."

With that, Tom leaned over and told Becky that he loved her. Becky wasn't sure that she wanted to tell Tom that she loved him. And she wasn't sure that she wanted to kiss him. But she *did* want to be engaged to him. So she whispered "I love you" to Tom and let him kiss her.

Tom was happy. He began to explain more about being engaged. "Always when we're coming to school or going home, we'll walk together—when nobody is looking, of course. At parties, I'll choose you and you'll choose me. Being engaged is so much fun. Why, Amy Lawrence and I—"

Becky's eyes grew large. She began to cry. "Oh, Tom! I'm not the first girl you've been engaged to!"

Tom tried, but he could not make Becky feel better. He gave her his greatest treasure: a brass doorknob. But Becky just threw it on the floor. Then Tom ran out of the room and over the hills. Becky ran after him, calling, "Tom! Come back, Tom!" But Tom did not return to school for the rest of the day.

4 Death in the Graveyard

Some time later, Tom was wandering through town when he saw Huckleberry Finn. Huck was hated by all the parents in the town. He didn't live in a house. He lived by himself on the streets. He didn't go to school. He did whatever he felt like doing. He dressed in old clothes that he found.

Like most boys in town, Tom liked Huck. He liked all the freedom that Huck had. Also like other boys, Tom had been told not to play with Huck. So he played with him whenever he could.

"Hello, Huckleberry!" called Tom.

"Hello, yourself, and see how you like it," answered Huck.

Huck was carrying a dead cat. "Let me see him, Huck," asked Tom. "My, he's pretty stiff. What are dead cats good for?"

"Good for? They can get rid of warts. You go to a graveyard at midnight and you say a special poem."

Huck told Tom that he was going to the graveyard that very night. Tom asked if he could go along. The two boys agreed that Huck would go to Tom's house late that night. Huck would wait outside and "meow." When Tom heard the sound, he would sneak out of the house.

At nine-thirty that night, Tom and Sid were sent to bed, as usual. Sid went right to sleep, but Tom stayed awake. Finally, after what seemed like forever, Tom heard a meow. He jumped up and climbed out the window. Huckleberry Finn was there with the dead cat.

It took them half an hour to walk to the graveyard. A soft wind groaned through the trees. The noises sounded like ghosts. The two boys didn't say much to each other. Finally, Tom turned to Huck and whispered, "Do you believe the dead people like us to be here?"

Huck whispered back, "I wish I knew. It seems so quiet and creepy here, doesn't it?"

Suddenly, Tom grabbed Huck's arm. "Sh!" The two boys held each other in fear. They heard some sounds. Then Huck said, "Lord, Tom! Ghosts are coming! What will we do?"

They saw three shadows. One was swinging an old lantern. Huck whispered to Tom, "It's ghosts all right. Three of them. Oh, Tom, we'll never get away. . . . Wait a minute! They're people! One of them is, anyway. I can hear old Muff Potter's voice. He's drunk, as usual."

Tom tried to see the men better. "We have to stay where we are, or they will see us. They're coming right this way. I know another one of those voices. It's Injun Joe."

The boys stopped talking. They both knew that no one liked or trusted Injun Joe. Before long, the three men stopped. They were standing within three feet of the boys' hiding place.

"Here it is," said the third voice. He lifted the lantern. The boys could see that it was Dr. Robinson. He sat down. He was very close to Huck and Tom. They could have touched him.

Injun Joe and Muff Potter began to dig up a grave. They took out a dead body and put it on a cart. Then Injun Joe said to Dr. Robinson, "Give us five dollars more, or we won't finish the job."

"I already paid you," answered Dr. Robinson. Injun Joe became angry. He said the doctor had to

pay for something that happened five years before. "Because of you, I was sent to jail for being a bum. I swore I'd get even with you if it took a hundred years! Now pay up." Injun Joe was talking and shaking his fist at the doctor. The doctor stood up and hit Injun Joe. Joe fell to the ground.

Potter ran up and said, "Don't hit my partner!" Dr. Robinson and Potter began to fight. But Potter was too drunk. The doctor knocked him down. Potter was out cold.

Suddenly, Injun Joe jumped up. He had Potter's knife! He ran up and stabbed Dr. Robinson. The doctor stumbled and fell on Potter. Blood spilled all over the drunk man's clothes. Injun Joe looked down at the doctor and said, "Now *that* score is settled."

By this time, the two scared boys were running away as fast as they could. They ran on and on, until they reached the town. They hid in an old shed. Each boy tried to catch his breath.

Tom was the first to speak. "Huck, what do you think is going to happen?"

"If Dr. Robinson dies, I guess Injun Joe will be hanged," answered Huck.

Tom thought for a while. Then he said, "Who is going to tell? Are we?"

"No, we can't tell. If we do, Injun Joe will kill us, too!" answered Huck.

So the two boys vowed never to tell anyone what they had seen that night.

By noon the next day, news of the murder was all over town. Muff Potter's knife had been found next to the body. Everyone was sure that he had killed Dr. Robinson.

All the town went to the graveyard. Tom didn't want to go back to that awful place. But he went along, anyway. It seemed like ages since he'd been there with Huck.

As Tom stood with the crowd, somebody pinched his arm. He turned and saw Huck. They gave each other a knowing look.

The crowd stood by the grave that had been dug up the night before. The doctor's body was still next to it. "Poor fellow," everyone said. But they didn't like the empty grave they saw. They all agreed that "this should be a lesson to grave robbers."

Just then, someone saw Muff Potter. "It's him! It's him! Don't let him get away!" A few men grabbed Potter.

Tom watched the crowd. Suddenly, he began to shake. Injun Joe was there. Joe told some people that he had seen the murder. But he told them that Muff Potter had stabbed Dr. Robinson. Potter didn't say anything. He had been too drunk to remember what had happened. The people believed Injun Joe. They took Potter to jail.

5 A Pirate with a Broken Heart

All the next week, Tom couldn't sleep well. He felt bad that he hadn't told people the truth. He wanted to clear Potter of the murder charge. But he knew what would happen if he did tell the truth. Injun Joe would kill him and Huck.

When Tom wasn't thinking about the murder, he was worrying about Becky Thatcher. She had stopped coming to school. He hadn't seen her since their fight.

For a few days, Tom tried to forget her. But he couldn't. Maybe she was sick! Maybe she would die! Tom stopped playing with his friends. He just moped around the schoolyard, hoping to see Becky.

Then, one day, she returned. Tom was happy. As soon as he saw Becky, Tom began playing games with his friends. He was yelling, laughing, chasing boys, and jumping over fences. He kept looking over at Becky. He wanted her to see him.

Becky *did* see Tom. But she didn't act the way he wanted. As she walked by him, she stuck her nose in the air. Then she said, "Some people think they're smart—always showing off!"

Tom was crushed. His mind was made up now. He was unloved. No one cared about him. He had no friends. He decided to live a life of crime. People had driven him to this. Yes, it was their fault. Maybe when he went away, they would be sorry.

After school, Tom took a walk in town. He saw his friend Joe Harper. Joe was also unhappy. His mother had gotten angry at him for drinking some cream. But he hadn't touched the cream!

Joe was feeling the way Tom was. It was plain that his mother was tired of him. Someday she would miss him. She had driven her boy out into the cold, hard world. There, he would suffer and die.

The two boys told each other their troubles. They promised to stand by each other. They would be brothers. They would never be apart until one of them died from his sufferings.

Tom talked Joe into running away to become a pirate. They found Huck Finn. He wanted to join them, too. The three boys agreed to meet that night at midnight. Each boy was to bring a fishing pole and some food.

At midnight, Tom arrived at the meeting place. All was quiet. He gave a low whistle. It was answered by another whistle. "Who goes there?" said a voice.

Tom used his best pirate voice. He whispered, "Tom Sawyer, Black Avenger of the Spanish Main. Name your names."

"Huck Finn, the Red Handed, and Joe Harper, the Terror of the Seas." Tom had found these names in his favorite book. He answered, "All is well. Give the secret password."

The other voices whispered, "BLOOD!"

The Black Avenger had brought a ham. The Terror of the Seas had brought a side of bacon. And Finn the Red Handed had stolen a frying pan. He also brought corn cobs for making pipes. But he was the only one who smoked.

The three pirates found a raft. On the raft, they found what was left of a smoking fire. This was handy, because the boys had no matches. They took the raft three miles down to a small island.

When they got to the island, they gathered some wood and built a fire. Then they cooked some bacon. After eating, they sat back to talk.

Huck asked Tom, "What do pirates have to do?"

"Oh, they have a great time," Tom explained. "They take ships and burn them. They steal the money and bury it in different places. They kill everyone on the ships—they make them walk a plank."

The boys talked more about the adventures they would have as pirates. Then they began to feel tired. Just before they fell asleep, the boys started to feel bad. But they didn't talk about it. They just thought about it. They wondered if it had been wrong to run away. And they thought about the food they had stolen.

They didn't really think about what they would do as pirates. But each boy promised himself one thing. As long as he was a pirate, he would not steal anything ever again.

When Tom awoke in the morning, he wondered where he was. Then he remembered. Everything was very quiet around him. He looked up. The raft was gone. "The wind must have blown it back into the river," thought Tom.

He woke up the other boys, and they all went swimming. After their swim, the boys felt hungry. Joe began to cut bacon for breakfast. Tom and Huck told Joe to wait. They grabbed their fishing poles and ran off.

A little while later, Tom and Huck returned with lots of fish. Joe cooked bacon and fish for breakfast. All three boys agreed on one thing: This was the best breakfast they had ever tasted!

After breakfast, the boys explored the island. They found that it was about three miles long. It was less than a mile wide. A sand bar at one end reached halfway across the river. Every hour, the boys went swimming. When they got hungry, they ate cold ham.

At first, this adventure was exciting. But soon, the boys stopped talking and exploring. They grew very quiet. Each boy was beginning to feel a little homesick. But they were all ashamed of their

"weakness." None was brave enough to say what he was thinking.

That afternoon, there was a sound in the distance. It was the boom of a cannon. It sounded once. Then it was silent. Then there was another boom.

"What is it?" asked Joe.

The boys thought for a minute. "It can't be thunder," said Huck. "Thunder is different. It—"

"I know!" said Tom. "Somebody has drowned."

"That's it!" agreed Huck. "They did that last year when Bill Turner drowned. I'd love to know who it is this time!"

The boys listened for a while. Then Tom had a thought. "I know who drowned," he said. "It's us! They think we're dead!"

The boys felt like heroes. The sounds showed that people missed them. People must feel bad. Hearts were breaking all over town. People were crying. Best of all, the boys were the talk of the town. They were famous. It was great to be a pirate, after all.

They swam and played the rest of the day. But, as the sun went down, the boys felt homesick again. Joe tried to talk a little about it. But Tom and Huck laughed at him. No one would say the truth. They all felt homesick. They all wanted to go home. Even Huck, who didn't have a real home.

After Joe and Huck fell asleep, Tom got up. He wrote a note on a piece of tree bark. He put it in Joe's hat. He also took things out of his pocket—a lump of chalk, a rubber ball, three fish hooks, and a special marble. He put all of these things in Joe's hat.

Then he ran toward the sand bar.

6 Tom's Visit Home

On the sand bar, Tom walked halfway across the river toward the shore. Then he swam the rest of the way. A short while later, he sneaked on a ferry that was going toward his town. Near town, he jumped off the ferry before anyone saw him.

Soon, after walking through back alleys, Tom was at his aunt's back fence. He climbed over. He saw a candle burning in the sitting room. He looked in the window. There sat Aunt Polly, Sid, and Joe Harper's mother. They were sitting by the bed. The bed was between them and the door.

Tom went to the door. He lifted the latch and pushed slowly. The door opened a little. Tom continued to push carefully. He got on his hands and knees. When the door was open wide enough, he began to sneak inside.

Just then, Aunt Polly said, "What makes the candle blow so much? Is the door open?"

When Tom heard that, he began to hurry. Aunt Polly turned around. "Yes, the door is open," she said. "A lot of strange things seem to be happening. Sid, go and shut the door."

Tom got under the bed just in time. He lay still for a while. He was trying to stop breathing so

hard. Then he crept to where he could almost touch Aunt Polly's foot.

"As I was saying, he wasn't really bad," began Aunt Polly. "He was just tricky. He was always getting into trouble. But he never meant any harm. He was a good-hearted boy."

Mrs. Harper nodded her head. "It was that way with my Joe, too," she explained. "He was always full of the devil. He was always up to something. But he really was a kind boy. And to think I got mad at him for taking that cream! I forgot that I had thrown it out because it was sour. Now I'll never see my boy again." Mrs. Harper cried as if her heart would break.

"I hope Tom is better off where he is," said Sid. "Of course, if he had been better in some ways—"

"Sid!" cried Aunt Polly. Tom couldn't see her. But he knew what kind of look she was giving Sid. "Not a word against my Tom, now that he's gone! Oh, Mrs. Harper! I don't know how to give him up! He was such a comfort to me—even if he did give me so much trouble."

Mrs. Harper sighed. "Well, the Lord giveth, and the Lord taketh away. But it's so hard! Only last Saturday, Joe lit a firecracker right next to me. I really let him have it! Little did I know then that he would be gone. Oh, I wish I had it to do over again. I'd hug him and bless him for it."

Aunt Polly nodded her head. "Yes, yes. I know just how you feel, Mrs. Harper," she said. "Just yesterday, I gave some medicine to Tom. He didn't want to take it. So he gave it to the cat. I thought the animal would tear the house down. I gave Tom such a hard time. Oh, the poor dead boy!"

This memory was too much for the woman. She broke down and cried. Even Tom was sniffling by now. He felt more sorry for himself than anyone else.

But Tom did feel bad that his aunt was so sad. He wanted to rush out from under the bed. It would make Aunt Polly so happy to see him still alive. But he just lay still and listened.

Tom heard how he and Joe had died. At first, people thought they had drowned while swimming. Then they saw that the raft was missing. Everyone had thought Tom and Joe would show up in the next town down the river. But then the raft was found the next day. It was on the shore, five miles from town.

Everyone was sure that the boys had taken the raft. And that they had somehow fallen off and drowned. After all, if they were alive, they would have come home once they got hungry.

People looked for the bodies for a while. Then they gave up. This was Wednesday night. If the bodies were still missing by Sunday, all hope would be gone. On Sunday, a funeral would be held. Tom felt strange hearing about his own funeral.

Mrs. Harper was still crying when she got up to leave. She said good night to Aunt Polly and Sid. She turned to go. Suddenly, the two women fell into each other's arms. They hugged each other and cried together. Then Mrs. Harper left the house.

Aunt Polly said good night to Sid. Then she knelt down to pray. She prayed for Tom. She sounded very sad. By the time her prayers were finished, Tom was crying.

Aunt Polly went to bed. But she had trouble falling asleep. She cried and turned over many times. Tom had to keep still under the bed.

At last, Aunt Polly was quiet. Tom sneaked out from under the bed. He picked up a candle and stood next to his aunt. He felt sorry for her. He thought of letting her know that he was alive.

But then Tom had an idea. He smiled. He bent over and kissed Aunt Polly. He left the house quickly.

It took Tom a long time to get back to the island. He used a rowboat for a while. He wanted to take it all the way to the island. But then, people might find him and his friends. So he left it at the side of the river, about a mile from the sand bar.

It was daylight when Tom reached the island. He walked up to the camp. He heard Joe say, "No, Huck. Tom is true-blue. He'll come back. He knows that running off would make him a bad pirate. Tom is too proud for that. I'll bet he's up to something. I wonder what."

Huck looked at the things Tom had left behind. "Well, these things are ours now, aren't they?"

"Pretty near, but not yet," answered Joe. "The note says we can have them if Tom isn't back for breakfast."

"Which he is!" yelled Tom, as he walked out of the bushes.

The boys had a delicious breakfast of fish and bacon. As they cooked it, Tom told Joe and Huck where he had been. He told them most of what he had heard. They all felt proud and famous.

Then Tom slept for a while. The other pirates got ready to fish and explore some more.

7 Pirates at Their Own Funeral

That afternoon, the boys hunted for turtle eggs. They poked sticks into the sand. When they found a soft place, they stopped. Then they got on their knees and dug with their hands. Sometimes, they found fifty or sixty eggs in one hole. Each egg was about the size of a walnut. The boys ate fried eggs that night and again on Friday morning.

The pirates spent Friday playing games. They chased each other, went swimming, and played marbles. They also pretended that they were clowns in a circus.

By the afternoon, the boys felt homesick again. Each one kept looking toward land. They couldn't see the town. But they knew where it was.

Tom lay on his back on the sand. He found himself writing "BECKY" with his big toe. Then he scratched it out. He was angry at himself. He thought he was being weak. But he wrote the name again, anyway. He couldn't help it.

Joe was so homesick that he felt like crying. Huck was unhappy, too. So was Tom, but he tried hard not to show it.

Finally, Joe said, "Come on, boys. Let's give it up. I want to go home."

"Oh, no, Joe. You'll feel better soon," answered Tom. "Just think of the swimming and fishing here."

"I don't care for fishing," said Joe. "And I don't seem to care for swimming. It's more fun when someone says that I can't do it. I want to go home."

Tom started laughing. "You baby! You want to see your mother!"

"Yes, I do want to see my mother," answered Joe. "You would, too, if you had one. I'm not any more of a baby than you are."

"Well, let's let the crybaby go home to his mother. Right, Huck? You and I will stay, won't we?" said Tom.

Huck said yes. But his heart wasn't in it.

Joe stood up. "I'll never speak to you as long as I live," he told Tom.

"Who cares!" answered Tom. But he felt bad.

Joe headed into the water. Tom's heart sank. He looked at Huck. Huck wouldn't look at him.

Then Huck said, "I want to go, too, Tom. It's too lonely out here. Let's go with Joe."

But Tom wouldn't give in. "I won't go," he yelled. "You can both go, if you want to. I plan to stay."

Huck followed Joe into the water. The water was shallow. They waded through it. Huck turned around. He called out to Tom. "I wish you would come, too. Think it over. We'll wait for you when we get to shore."

"Well, you'll wait a long time!" screamed Tom. But he really wanted to go with his friends. He hoped the boys would stop. But they kept going. Finally, Tom ran into the water. He yelled, "Wait! Wait! I want to tell you something!"

Huck and Joe stopped. Tom hurried toward them. He told them his secret. It was the idea that had come to him when he saw Aunt Polly sleeping. Huck and Joe didn't say much. Then they got the "point" of what Tom was saying. They laughed and clapped. They said the idea was "great!" They told Tom that he should have told them sooner. Then they wouldn't have wanted to leave.

So the three pirates stayed on the island. The next day, they continued their adventures. They did much the same as on the other days. But now they had a secret. It made them feel that they were having more fun.

But there was no fun in the town on that Saturday. The families of Joe and Tom were very sad. They cried many tears.

In the afternoon, Becky Thatcher was alone. She walked to the schoolhouse. "If only I had kept the brass doorknob Tom gave me," she said to herself. "Now I have nothing to remember him by."

She walked around a little. She came to the spot where she had called Tom a show-off. "It was right here," she cried. "Oh, I wish I had it to do over again. I wouldn't say that for the world. But he's gone now. I'll never, never see him again." She walked away, crying.

A group of boys came by. They were talking about how Tom used to do so-and-so, and how Joe used to say this-and-that. Each boy remembered when he had last seen the dead boys. There were arguments over who was the last person to see Tom or Joe.

One boy bragged that Tom had beaten him in a fight once. But this was nothing special. Most of the boys could say that.

On Sunday morning, the church bell rang. It was time for the funeral.

The minister stood in the church. He talked about Tom and Joe. The people in the church were unhappy. They were sorry that Tom and Joe were dead. The minister said many good things about the boys. Most of the people felt bad, because they didn't remember the boys being so good.

The speech continued. The minister told some stories about Tom and Joe. He talked about how sweet and kind the boys had been. Before long, everyone in the church was crying.

There was a noise upstairs. Nobody heard it. A moment later, the church door opened. The minister looked up from his handkerchief. He stopped crying and talking. He just stood there, staring at the back of the church.

One by one, people turned around. They wanted to see what the minister was looking at. One by one, the people stood up and stared.

The three dead boys came walking up the aisle. Tom was in front. Behind him was Joe. Huck was last. They had been hiding upstairs. They had listened to their own funeral!

Aunt Polly and the Harpers threw themselves on Tom and Joe. They kept hugging and kissing the two boys. Huck stood watching. No one paid attention to him.

As Huck started to leave, Tom grabbed him. Tom turned to Aunt Polly and said, "Somebody has to be glad to see Huck!"

"I'll be glad to see Huck," Aunt Polly cried. "After all, he has no mother of his own!" She began kissing and hugging Huck.

Suddenly everyone in the church started singing. Tom Sawyer the Pirate looked around him. All this attention was for him! He could see that his friends were jealous. He was happy. This was the proudest moment in his life. His idea had worked perfectly!

8 Tom Takes Becky's Punishment

On Tom's first day back at school, he was a hero. All his schoolmates wanted to know about his adventures.

Tom liked all this attention. It made him feel that he didn't need Becky Thatcher. He could live without her. He was sure that now Becky would want to make up with him. He decided that he didn't care.

Soon Becky came by with some of her friends. She was laughing and playing. She didn't say anything to Tom. But he could see that she kept playing close to where he was. She kept looking over at him, but Tom acted as if he didn't know that Becky was there. He was talking to Amy Lawrence.

Becky was standing very close to Tom. She began talking to her friends. "My mom is going to let me have a picnic," she announced.

"Oh, won't that be fun!" answered one girl. "Will you invite all the girls and boys in class?"

Becky looked at Tom. "I'll ask everyone who is my friend—or who wants to be," she answered.

Tom didn't even look at her. Soon everyone in the group had asked to be invited. Everyone, that is, except Tom and Amy. They kept talking to each other. Then they just walked away.

Becky felt like crying, but she kept talking and laughing. But now the picnic wasn't important. Nothing seemed important.

At recess, Tom continued to talk with Amy. He wanted Becky to feel worse. At first, he couldn't find her. But then he saw her. She was sitting with Alfred Temple on a small bench. They were looking at a picture book.

Tom was red-hot with jealousy. Amy kept talking to him. But Tom didn't hear what she was saying. He didn't answer any of her questions. He was angry and upset. Becky didn't seem to know he was alive. He left Amy and went home for lunch.

Becky *did* know that Tom was alive. But she knew that she was winning the fight. Tom had made her suffer. Now he could suffer.

Becky sat with Alfred during lunch. She waited for Tom to come back. But he didn't return. Finally, Becky grew unhappy. She wished that she had ended the fight with Tom. She turned to Alfred and cried, "Oh, don't bother me! I don't care about these pictures! Go away and leave me alone!"

Alfred was surprised. He wondered what he'd done wrong. Becky had said that they would look at pictures all during lunch. Then Alfred thought about Tom Sawyer. He knew that Becky had used him to make Tom angry.

Alfred tried to think of a way to get even with Tom. He walked into the classroom. When he saw Tom's spelling book, Alfred had an idea. He opened the book to the lesson for that afternoon. He poured ink all over the page.

Becky was looking in the window at that moment. She saw what Alfred did. She started to walk to Tom's house. She was going to tell Tom what Alfred had done. But she changed her mind. She remembered how Tom had acted when she talked about her picnic. She decided to let Tom get in trouble.

Tom almost played hooky that afternoon. But then he decided to return to school. He saw Becky outside the school. She was alone. Tom walked up to her and said, "I acted pretty mean today, Becky. I'm sorry. I won't ever act that way again. Please make up, won't you?"

The girl stopped and looked at him. Then she said, "Just keep yourself to yourself, Mr. Tom Sawyer. I'll never speak to you again."

She tossed her head and walked away. Tom was so surprised that he didn't say anything. As soon as Becky was gone, he thought about it. He could have said, "So, who cares, Miss Smarty?" But he didn't think of that soon enough.

Tom walked into school. He passed Becky and said something mean. She yelled something mean at him. They were now enemies.

Becky looked forward to seeing Tom get in trouble. But she didn't know that she would soon be in big trouble, also.

Mr. Dobbins was the schoolteacher. All his life he had wanted to be a doctor. But he became a teacher instead. He still thought about being a doctor. He kept a science book in his desk drawer. Each day, he waited until the students were working. Then he took out this book and read it. When he finished reading, he always locked the book in the drawer.

The students were dying to know what the book was about. On this day, Becky was the first person in the classroom after lunch. The teacher's desk was by the door. Becky walked by the desk. The key was in the drawer!

Becky looked around. She was alone. She opened the drawer. In a moment, she had the book in her hands. The book was by some doctor. Becky read the title: *Anatomy.* She didn't know what that was. So she began to turn the pages. Right away, she came upon a picture. It was a human figure, naked.

Just then, a shadow fell on the page. Tom Sawyer stepped inside the door. He saw the picture. Becky rushed to close the book. By accident, she tore the picture in half. She threw the book into the desk and closed the drawer.

"You should be ashamed of yourself, Tom Sawyer!" she cried. "I know you'll tell on me. What

will I do? I've never gotten in trouble in school before. You are mean and hateful!" She started crying and ran out of the room.

Tom stood still. He was surprised that Becky was so upset. He said to himself, "So what if she's going to get in trouble? It happens to me all the time. But I won't tell old Dobbins. Dobbins will find out who did it on his own. He will ask who tore the book. Nobody will answer. Then he'll do what he always does. He will ask each of us separately. When he gets to Becky, he'll know. Her face will tell on her. There just isn't any way out of it."

Shortly after class started, Tom got in trouble because of his spelling book. He wasn't too unhappy about it. He thought that maybe he did spill the ink and had forgotten about it. Of course, he told Mr. Dobbins that he hadn't done it.

Becky was a little surprised at how she felt. She thought that she would be glad when Tom got in trouble. But she found that she wasn't so sure. She almost stood up and told on Alfred Temple. But she made herself keep quiet. She said to herself, "Tom would tell on me for tearing the book anyway. I wouldn't say a word, even to save his life."

An hour passed. The students were working. Mr. Dobbins opened his desk and took out his book. Most of the students looked up at him. Then they returned to their work. But two students watched Mr. Dobbins very carefully. In a minute, the teacher was on his feet. He faced the students and asked, "Who tore this book?"

There was no answer. Mr. Dobbins began to do what Tom knew he would do.

"Joe Harper, did you tear this book?"

Joe said that he didn't.

"Amy Lawrence, did you tear this book?"

She shook her head.

Tom looked at Becky. She was the next girl to be asked. Her face was white with terror.

Mr. Dobbins looked at Becky. "Becky Thatcher, look me in the face. Did you tear this book?"

A thought shot through Tom's mind. Suddenly, he jumped up. He shouted, "I did it!"

The students stared at Tom. They were surprised. They couldn't believe that he would admit to doing something like that.

But Tom was happy. He didn't mind being punished. He could see the grateful look on Becky's face. He didn't even mind staying after school for two hours. He knew who would wait for him.

When Tom went to bed that night, he thought about how he would get back at Alfred Temple. Becky had told him about Alfred spilling ink on the spelling book. But soon Tom began thinking of nicer things. He fell asleep with Becky's words in his mind: "Oh, Tom! How could you be so wonderful!"

9 Muff Potter's Trial

At last, the murder trial was about to begin. Everyone in town was talking about it. Tom could not get away from it. Every time someone spoke of the murder, Tom shook with fear.

One day, Tom had a talk with Huck. "Have you told anyone about you-know-what?" Tom asked.

"Of course I haven't," Huck answered. "We wouldn't be alive two days if we told anyone. Injun Joe would kill us for sure. You know that."

Tom felt better. Now he knew for sure that Huck wouldn't tell anyone. But he was still a little worried. "Huck, they couldn't get someone to make you tell, could they?"

Huck shook his head. "Get me to tell? If I wanted Injun Joe to drown me, they could get me to tell. There's no other way."

So the boys promised again not to tell anyone about the murder. But, after a while, they thought about poor Muff Potter. They felt bad that he was in jail.

"Muff is drunk most of the time," said Huck. "But he doesn't hurt anyone. He fishes a little and drinks a lot. But he's really nice. Once he gave me half of his fish. He didn't really have enough to eat. But he shared what he had with me."

Tom also remembered how nice Potter had been to him. "He has fixed kites for me. And he taught me how to put bait on a fish hook."

The boys decided to visit Muff Potter in jail. They stood outside the window and passed some cigarettes and matches to Potter.

"You boys sure have been nice to me," Potter said. "I thank you for it. I've been saying to myself that I used to do things for all the boys in town. They were my friends then. But now all the boys have forgotten me. All except Tom and Huck. They don't forget me. I want to thank you both for still being my friends."

Tom went home feeling terrible. He had dreams about Muff Potter being hanged.

The trial started the next morning. Tom thought of going to watch it. But he forced himself to stay away. He stayed away from Huck, too. Seeing Huck would just make Tom feel worse.

On the second day of the trial, people in town were still talking about it. They knew that Potter would be found guilty. Injun Joe had been a witness. He still said that Muff Potter had killed the doctor.

Tom was out late that night. He came to bed through the bedroom window. He was very excited. It took hours for him to fall asleep.

The courtroom was packed the next day. Everyone knew this would be the last day of the trial.

A witness was called. He said that he saw Muff Potter on the day after the murder. It was early in the morning. Potter was washing himself in the river.

Then it was time for Potter's lawyer to ask questions. But the lawyer just said, "I have no questions."

The next witness told about finding Potter's knife near the dead body. Again, Potter's lawyer had his turn to ask questions. Again, he said, "I have no questions."

The same thing happened with all the witnesses. People in the courtroom started to whisper. They were not happy. Would this lawyer just throw away Potter's life without a fight?

Then it was time for Potter's lawyer to call *his* witnesses. He stood up and said, "At first, I told the court that Mr. Potter did kill Dr. Robinson. I said I would prove that Mr. Potter was too drunk to know what he was doing. But I have changed my mind. Instead, I call Tom Sawyer to the witness stand!"

All the people in the courtroom were surprised. What could Tom know? Everyone looked at Tom. He was shaking as he walked to the witness stand. He was scared.

The lawyer asked Tom, "Where were you at midnight on the seventeenth of June?"

At first, Tom was too afraid to say anything. He looked at Injun Joe. The room was quiet. Then Tom said, "In the graveyard!"

A smile came to Injun Joe's face. He looked as if he wasn't worried.

"Was anyone else with you?" asked the lawyer.

"Yes," said Tom. "It was—"

"No, don't tell us now," said the lawyer. "If we need to, we will talk to that person later. Now, Tom, were you anywhere near the grave that was dug up that night?"

"Yes, sir," answered Tom. "We were behind the trees that are next to the grave."

Injun Joe frowned. He leaned forward to listen.

The lawyer wanted Tom to continue. "Now, my boy, tell us everything that happened," he said. "Tell it in your own way. Don't skip anything, and don't be afraid."

Tom began to talk. He spoke slowly at first. But then he began to tell the story quickly. Every eye in the room was on him. Nobody made a sound.

Finally, Tom reached the important part of his story. He said "—and the doctor knocked down Muff Potter. Then Injun Joe jumped up with the knife and—"

Crash! Quick as lightning, Injun Joe jumped for the window. He pushed people out of his way and was gone!

10 Looking for Buried Treasure

Tom was a hero once again. He even had his name in the town newspaper. His days were fun and exciting.

But Tom's nights were different. Injun Joe was in all his dreams. Tom stopped climbing out of his bedroom window at night.

Huck was just as upset as Tom. Tom had told the lawyer the whole story. After Injun Joe's escape, the lawyer had promised not to tell anyone that Huck was part of it. But, who could be sure? Maybe the lawyer had told someone.

Tom tried not to think about Injun Joe during the day. One day, he decided that he wanted to dig for buried treasure. He asked Joe Harper, but Joe couldn't go. So Tom found Huck and asked him to go. Huck was always interested in adventures.

"Where will we dig?" asked Huck.

"Oh, most anywhere," answered Tom. "Treasure is hidden in very special places. Sometimes on islands. Sometimes in rotten chests under old dead trees. Most of the time, it's hidden under the floor in haunted houses."

"Who hides it?" asked Huck.

"Well, robbers, of course," said Tom. "Who do you think hides it? Sunday-school teachers?"

"I don't know," answered Huck. "If it were mine, I wouldn't hide it. I'd spend it and have fun."

"So would I," agreed Tom. "But robbers don't do it that way. They always hide it and leave it there. They think they'll come back for it. But they forget, or else they die. It just lies there. After a long time, someone finds an old yellow paper. The paper has marks that show where the treasure is."

"Have you got one of those papers, Tom?" asked Huck.

"No. But the robbers always bury the treasure under an old tree or under a haunted house. There's the old haunted house up on Still-House Hill. And there are lots of old trees around it. We can try those trees first."

"But, that could take all summer!" said Huck.

"Well, so what?" answered Tom. "We might find a pot with a hundred dollars in it. Or a big chest full of diamonds."

Huck's eyes grew big. "All right, let's do it," he said.

The two boys found an old pick and a shovel. Then they walked three miles to Still-House Hill. When they got there, they were hot and tired. They lay under a tree to rest.

"Say, Huck, what if we find treasure here? What will you do with your share?" asked Tom.

Huck smiled and said, "I'll have pie and a glass of soda every day. I'll go to every circus that comes to town. I'll have a great time. What will you do, Tom?"

"I'm going to buy a new drum, a real sword, and a red necktie," answered Tom.

The boys agreed that it was time to start working. They chose a tree and began to dig. They dug for half an hour. They found nothing. They dug for another half an hour. Still, they found nothing. Then they chose a new spot and began again.

Finally, the boys stopped digging. They were hot and tired. Tom thought for a minute. Then he said, "I know what the problem is! We have to come at midnight. Then we look for a dead tree. We're supposed to dig in the shadow of the branch of a dead tree!"

That night, Tom heard a meow outside his window. He climbed out to meet Huck. They went back to Still-House Hill. They dug in the shadow of a branch of a dead tree. But they found nothing.

Finally, Huck stopped digging. "Let's try somewhere else."

The boys agreed to try the haunted house. Of course, they couldn't go into the house at night. They didn't want to meet any ghosts. They leaned their tools against the tree. Then they made plans to meet the next day.

At about noon the next day, Tom and Huck arrived at the dead tree. They picked up their tools and walked to the haunted house.

When they reached the house, they were afraid to go in. They sneaked up to the door. They peeked in. They saw a living room with a big fireplace. The room didn't have a floor. Weeds were growing all over the ground. There were cobwebs hanging everywhere.

Tom and Huck entered slowly. They spoke in whispers. They began to explore the house. As they got used to being there, they became less scared.

They decided to go upstairs. They leaned their tools against a wall. Then they walked upstairs. They looked in all the rooms. Suddenly, Tom whispered, "Sh!"

The boys froze. "What is it?" asked Huck.

They both heard noises. "Keep still!" ordered Tom. "Don't move. Someone's coming to the front door."

Tom and Huck lay on the floor. There were cracks in the old floor. The boys looked through the cracks at the room below.

Two men entered the front door. Both Tom and Huck had seen one of the men before. Both boys were thinking, "That's the old deaf-and-dumb man that has been hanging around town lately." He was wrapped in a serape and was wearing a sombrero. He had long white hair and whiskers, and he was wearing dark glasses.

The other man was ragged and dirty. He was speaking in a low voice. "No," he said. "I've thought it over. I don't like it. Another robbery would be too dangerous."

"Dangerous!" grunted the "deaf-and-dumb" man. "Baloney!"

The boys were surprised to hear him speak. They were also scared. The voice was Injun Joe's!

The two men continued talking. They took out some food and ate lunch. After lunch, Injun Joe said, "I'm dead for sleep! It's your turn to watch."

He curled up in the weeds. Soon he began to snore. Before long, the other man was also snoring.

The boys upstairs drew a long breath. Tom whispered, "Now is our chance—come on!"

But Huck held back. He was afraid that the men would wake up. Tom stood up slowly. He started to walk to the stairs. His first step made the floor creak loudly. Tom sank down onto the floor. He was almost dead with fear. He didn't try again. The boys lay there for hours.

Finally, one snore stopped. Injun Joe sat up and looked around. Then he kicked his partner. "Some watchman you are!" said Joe. "It's all right, though—nothing has happened. What should we do with the money we have?"

"I don't know," answered the other man. "Let's leave it here. We can come get it before we go away. It's hard to carry $650 in silver. But let's bury it deep, just in case."

The boys forgot their fear. With $650, they would be rich! This would be a great way to find a treasure. They would know just where to dig for it!

They watched as Injun Joe took out his knife. He dug a hole in front of the fireplace.

Just then, Joe's knife hit something. "What's this?" he asked. He reached down into the hole with his hand. He pulled out a handful of coins. They were gold. The boys upstairs were as excited as the men downstairs.

The other man looked around. Then he said, "I saw an old shovel by the door. Let's dig up this money."

Soon the box was out of the hole. In it were thousands of dollars in gold coins. The two men began to bury the box again. They planned to come back for it later. Huck and Tom thought that was a great idea.

But then, Injun Joe changed his mind. "No, we can't leave it here," he said. "That shovel had fresh dirt on it. Why was it here? Who brought it here? Where has the person gone? We can't leave the money here. The person who owns the shovel will come back. He'll see that we've been digging."

The two men decided to take all the money with them. Injun Joe put away his knife. He said that he would hide the coins "under the cross" in his secret hiding place.

Then Injun Joe stood up. He started walking around, looking out the windows. He turned to his friend and said, "Who could have brought that shovel here? Do you think they might be upstairs?"

Tom and Huck held their breaths. They were sick with fear. Injun Joe put his hand on his knife. He walked to the stairway and began to walk upstairs.

Tom and Huck thought of trying to hide in the closet. But they were too scared to move. Then they got back their strength. They got ready to stand up.

Suddenly, there was a crash of rotten wood. Injun Joe landed on the ground under the broken staircase. He stood up. He was angry.

The other man said, "Let's forget it. If they're up there, let them stay. If they want to jump down and give us trouble, let them try. We have to get going. It's almost dark. Let them try to follow us if they want."

Injun Joe agreed with his friend. They picked up the box of gold and walked out of the house.

Tom and Huck stood up. They felt weak. They were glad the men were leaving. Follow them? Not these boys. They just wanted to get out of the house without breaking their necks.

Tom and Huck didn't talk much. They were angry at themselves. They should have left the shovel by the tree. Then Injun Joe wouldn't have worried. He would have left the gold there. Tom and Huck would have been rich.

The sorry treasure hunters left the house and headed for home.

11 Adventures in the Cave

Becky Thatcher decided to have the picnic she had talked about. It was planned for the following Saturday.

Saturday morning came, and everyone was excited. The Thatchers had rented a ferryboat. The boat would take all the children down the river. The picnic would be held in the forest three miles from town.

Becky's parents were not going to the picnic. Instead, they were sending a younger couple to watch over the children. Mrs. Thatcher said to Becky, "You might not get back until late. Maybe you should stay overnight with someone who lives near the boat dock." Becky told her mother that she would stay with her friend Susy Harper. Then she went outside to meet Tom.

As they walked to the ferryboat, Tom turned to Becky. "I have an idea," he said. "Don't go to Susy Harper's house. We can both go to the Widow Douglas's house. She will have ice cream! She has it almost every day. She'd be glad to have us stay over. Living alone as she does, she's always glad to have company."

Becky liked the idea. But what would her mother say? Tom had an answer to her question. "Your mother just wants you to be safe. We'll be safe with Mrs. Douglas. Your mother might have told you to go there, if she had thought of it!" So Tom and Becky decided to follow this plan.

They soon joined all the other children on the ferryboat. When the boat arrived down the river at the forest, the children ran off and began playing games. After some time they were all tired, and they ate lunch. Then they sat in the shade and talked. By and by, someone shouted, "Who's ready for the cave?"

Everyone was ready. Each child was given a candle. Then the children ran up the hill to the cave. The opening to the cave was shaped like the letter A. Inside, the cave was as cold as an icehouse.

The children lit their candles and began to explore. The main hallway of the cave was about eight or ten feet wide. Every few steps, there were smaller alleys and rooms on both sides. Many of these alleys ran into each other. Most of them went nowhere at all.

It was said that a person could walk around for days and never find the end of the cave. Most people knew a little part of it. They didn't go farther than the parts they knew. Tom Sawyer knew as much of the cave as anyone else did.

The group walked down the main hallway. They were laughing and playing. They explored the small rooms on the sides of the hallway. Sometimes, someone would slip into one of the little rooms. Then that person would jump out in front of the whole group.

One by one, the explorers went back to the cave opening, talking and laughing. They were out of breath. They were surprised that so much time had been spent in the cave. It was sunset already. The group returned to the ferryboat. The boat began its journey home.

The next day was Sunday. Mrs. Thatcher saw Mrs. Harper in church. "Is my Becky going to sleep all day?" asked Mrs. Thatcher. "I'm sure she is tired to death."

Mrs. Harper looked surprised. "Your Becky?" she said.

Mrs. Thatcher opened her eyes wide. "Yes, didn't she stay with you?" When Mrs. Harper said no, Mrs. Thatcher turned pale. She sat down.

Just then, Aunt Polly walked by. "Good morning, Mrs. Thatcher. Good morning, Mrs. Harper," she said. "My boy has turned up missing. I guess my Tom stayed at your house last night—one of you. And now he's afraid to come to church. I need to talk to that boy."

"He didn't stay with us," answered Mrs. Harper.

"I haven't seen him, either," said Mrs. Thatcher.

Before long, everyone in town knew that the two children were missing. None of the other children could remember if Becky and Tom were on the ferryboat going home.

Finally, one boy said out loud what everyone was thinking. Maybe Tom and Becky were lost in the cave. Mrs. Thatcher fainted. Aunt Polly began to cry.

All afternoon, the town seemed empty and dead. Most of the men had gone to the cave. Most of the women had stayed behind. They tried to comfort Aunt Polly and Mrs. Thatcher.

The search went on all night. The only news came in the early morning: "Send more candles—and send food."

Now we should return to Tom and Becky. What happened to them? They were playing in the cave along with everyone else. But after a while, they became tired of all the games. They wanted to see more of the cave.

They began to walk down one of the alleys next to the main hallway. They saw that many people had used candle smoke to write on the walls. Tom and Becky read all these names, dates, and messages. They added their names to the wall.

Tom found a small natural staircase. He wanted to explore it. Becky was willing, so they walked down it together. They walked back and forth, finding more new hallways and rooms. Once in a while, they made marks on the cave walls. This way, they would know how to get out.

Then something happened. They found a group of sleeping bats. When the bats saw the candles, they flew at Tom and Becky. Tom grabbed Becky's hand. They ran and ran. They escaped the bats. But then they looked around.

Becky was the first to speak. "I didn't think of this before. It's been a long time since I heard the others. I hope we're not lost."

The two children walked through some hall-ways and rooms, looking for the marks they had made. Tom kept saying, "Oh, it's all right. We'll find the way very soon."

But he felt less and less hopeful each time they entered a strange room. Finally, he said, "I can't find the way. It's all mixed up."

Becky sat down on the ground. She started to cry. Tom held her. He said everything he could think of to stop her from crying. But she kept crying.

Then Tom began to blame himself for getting Becky lost. This was the best way to stop her from crying. She began to try to make him feel better. She told him they were both to blame. She agreed to help Tom find the way out.

They walked around for a while. But they couldn't find a way out. When they found an under-ground spring, they drank some water. They decid-ed to stay near the spring. They cried a little and fell asleep.

When Tom and Becky woke up, they were hun-gry. Tom took a piece of cake out of his pocket. He had saved it from the picnic. They shared it with-out talking.

Becky began to worry again. Again, Tom tried to make her feel better. He said he was sure that people would come looking for them. Becky won-dered when. "Your mother would miss you as soon as everyone got home from the picnic," explained Tom.

Becky looked frightened. Suddenly, Tom knew why. Becky was not going to go home that night! No one would come looking for them until the next day. The two children became very quiet. Before long, the last piece of candle burned out. Becky and Tom went to sleep again.

When Tom woke up, he had an idea. There were some hallways close by. He could explore some of them. He took a spool of kite string out of his pocket. He tied one end to a rock. Then he began to crawl. It was dark, so he had to move slowly. He went around a few corners, hoping to find something.

Suddenly, he saw a human hand. It was holding a candle. Tom shouted with joy. Then he saw who was holding the candle. It was Injun Joe!

Tom was so scared that he couldn't move. Luckily, Injun Joe was frightened by the yell. He turned around and ran away.

Still shaking, Tom went back to Becky. He didn't tell her about Injun Joe. He told her that he had shouted "for luck."

The children slept again. When they woke up, they were very hungry. There was no more cake. All they could do was drink water from the spring. They began to fear that nobody would find them.

Becky was very quiet. She was sure that she was going to die. She said that if Tom wanted to, he could explore some more. But Becky decided she would just lie down and wait to die.

Back at the town, it was a quiet Tuesday after-noon. Tom and Becky had been in the cave for three days. Mrs. Thatcher was very sick. Aunt Polly just sat and stared, and her gray hair had grown almost white.

But, in the middle of the night, a shout was heard. "They're found! They're found!" A parade of people were walking down Main Street. Tom and Becky were with them. All the lights of the town were on. Nobody went to bed for the rest of the night. It was the greatest night the town had ever had!

Everyone wanted to hear what had happened. Tom enjoyed telling the history of his adventure.

It seems that Tom had left Becky to explore. The kite string kept him from losing her. He was al-most at the end of the kite string. And he was about to turn back. Suddenly, he saw some light. He crawled to the light. It was a hole to the outside!

Tom hurried back to get Becky. Together, they crawled out the hole. They were on a hillside above the river. They waved to a passing boat. The men in the boat took Tom and Becky to a house and gave them some food. They made the children rest until two or three hours after dark. Then they took the two children to the town.

Three days and nights in the cave had been hard on Becky and Tom, as they soon found out. They were both sick in bed for many days. It took Becky five days before she could even leave her room. It was almost two weeks before Tom could go to see her. Finally, Tom went by the Thatcher house for a visit. Mr. Thatcher asked Tom if he'd want to go to that cave again. Tom said that he thought he wouldn't mind.

"Well, nobody will get lost in that cave ever again," said Mr. Thatcher. "Two weeks ago, I had the opening covered with an iron door. There are three locks on the door—and I've got the keys."

Tom's eyes grew big. He turned as white as a sheet. "Oh, no!" he cried. "Injun Joe is in the cave!"

Within a few minutes, the news had spread. A group of men got a boat and went to the cave. They unlocked the door.

Injun Joe lay stretched on the floor. He was dead. His face was close to the crack in the door. He looked as if he had been trying to get out.

Tom felt bad about how Injun Joe had died. Tom had been lost in the cave, too. He knew how Injun Joe must have suffered.

Tom felt bad, but he also felt relieved. He didn't have to be afraid anymore.

12 Floods of Gold

On the morning after Injun Joe's funeral, Tom went to see Huck. He took Huck to a quiet place to have a talk. "Huck, listen to me!" Tom said. "Injun Joe hid all that money in the cave!"

Huck's eyes lit up. "Are you sure, Tom?" he asked.

"I'm as sure as ever I was in my life," answered Tom. "Will you go there with me and help get it out? I just know it's there. If we don't find it, I'll give you my drum and everything I have in the world."

Huck was willing to go. But he wondered how they would get into the cave. "There's a locked door on the opening," explained Tom. "But I know a secret way in. If we row down the river, I'll know it when we get there."

So the boys got some supplies. They had sandwiches, candles, and some spools of kite string. They found a small rowboat that they could use for the afternoon.

Tom took the boat down the river. Then he said, "See the side of the hill? It looks like nothing from here. There are no houses. All the trees and bushes look alike. But can you see that spot where there was a landslide? That's one of the things I remember. The opening is up there."

The boys landed the boat. They walked up the hill. Tom asked Huck to try to find the cave opening. Huck looked all around. He couldn't see anything. Tom walked proudly up to a big bush. "Here you are!" he said. "It's a great hole. Don't tell anyone about it. I've always wanted to be a robber. But I needed a hideout like this. We'll just tell Joe Harper and Ben Rogers. There's got to be a gang, or there wouldn't be any style. Tom Sawyer's Gang—it sounds great, doesn't it?"

Huck agreed. But he wondered what kind of robbing they would do.

"Oh, mostly we'll take people," answered Tom.

"Will we kill them?" asked Huck.

"No, not always. We'll hide them until they raise a ransom," explained Tom.

"What's a ransom?" Huck asked.

"Money. You make them raise all they can from their friends. You keep them for a year. If you haven't got the money from them, you kill them. You don't hurt or kill the women. They're always beautiful and rich. And they're always scared. You take their watches and things. But you always take your hat off and talk nicely to them. Robbers are very polite. After the women have been in the cave for two weeks, they fall in love with you. Then they want to stay."

Huck agreed that it sounded exciting. "I think that's better than being a pirate," he added.

The boys entered the hole. They lit their candles. They tied the ends of their kite strings to a rock. Then they began to walk.

In a few minutes, they reached the spring. Tom shook a little, as he remembered being there with Becky. He showed Huck the little piece of candle. He explained how he and Becky had watched the flame die.

The cave was quiet. The boys didn't really like being there. Then Tom said, "Now I'll show you something, Huck."

Tom held his candle high. "Look as far around the corner as you can. Do you see that? There—on the big rock over there. See what's been written with candle smoke?"

"Tom, it's a cross!" cried Huck. He remembered what Injun Joe had said in the haunted house. He was taking the money to a place "under the cross."

The boys began to search. Tom went first. There were four hallways around the rock with the cross. The boys explored them. They found nothing.

They didn't know where to look next. "He said under the cross," said Huck. "This is the closest thing to being under the cross. It can't be under the rock itself. The rock is too heavy to move."

Tom started digging in the clay around the rock. When he had dug four inches down, he hit wood. Huck began to help dig.

Before long, the box of gold and silver coins sat in front of the boys. "We've got it at last, Tom," yelled Huck. "My goodness, we're rich!"

They tried to lift the box. It weighed about fifty pounds. Tom was glad that he had brought some bags. They put the money in the bags. Then they returned to the boat and rowed back to town.

The bags were heavy. When Tom and Huck got to town, they decided to use a friend's wagon to carry the coins. They hadn't gone far when someone ran up to them. There was a party at Mrs. Douglas's home! The boys thought about how they could tell everyone about the money. They hurried to the party.

At the party, people began talking about Huck. They were saying how sad it was that he didn't have a home. How hard it must be for a boy without parents.

Then Mrs. Douglas told Huck why she was having the party. She said that she had been thinking about him ever since he, Tom, and Joe had shown up at their own funeral. She said she wanted to give him a home because he didn't have anybody and neither did she. She would give him new clothes and send him to school. Someday she might have enough money to help him start a business.

This was Tom's chance to speak. "Huck doesn't need it. He's got money."

Everyone smiled. They knew that Huck was poor.

"Don't smile," Tom said. "I guess I'll just show you. Wait a minute."

He ran outside. When he came back in, he was carrying the bags. He emptied them on the table. "There, what did I tell you?" he cried. "Half of this is Huck's, and half of it is mine!"

Everyone was surprised. People didn't know what to say. They began to count the money. It was a little over $12,000. It was more money than anyone there had seen before.

13 Huck Joins Tom's Gang

Everyone in the town was interested in Tom and Huck's treasure. Every "haunted" house in the area was torn apart. Other people hoped to find a treasure. Most of these people were grown men—not young boys.

Mrs. Douglas put Huck's money in the bank. And Aunt Polly did the same with Tom's money. Each boy received a dollar a day. That was a lot of money in those days. Back then, a grown person could live for a whole week on a dollar and a quarter.

Mrs. Douglas kept her promise. She gave Huck Finn a home. She bought him new clothes and sent him to school. He slept in a real bed. He ate at a table and had to use a knife, fork, and napkin.

Huck lived at Mrs. Douglas's house for three weeks. One day, he disappeared. Mrs. Douglas and other people in town looked for him for two days.

On the third day, Tom took a walk. He had a feeling that he knew where to find Huck. Tom walked to the old shacks in the old part of town.

And that's where Huck was. He was eating some bits of food he had stolen. His hair was mussed and his face was dirty. He was wearing the old clothes he used to wear, and he had no shoes on.

Tom told Huck about how worried everyone was.
He told Huck that he should go home to Mrs.
Douglas.

Huck frowned. "Don't talk about it," he said to
Tom. "I tried it and it doesn't work. It isn't for me.
The old woman is nice to me, but I can't live like
that. She makes me get up at the same time every
morning. She makes me wash all the time. I have
to wear those awful clothes. I have to go to school. I
just can't do all that!"

"Well, everybody lives that way, Huck," answered Tom.

Huck wouldn't change his mind. "It doesn't make any difference. I'm not everybody, and I can't stand it. This is the way I like to live. And I'll tell you something else, Tom. I wouldn't be in all this trouble if it weren't for that money. I like the woods and the river, and I always will! Tell you what—you take my share of the money. I don't want it."

Tom thought of a way to change Huck's mind. "Look here, Huck. I still plan to be a robber, even though I'm rich. But we can't let you into the gang if you don't live like everybody else."

"You can't let me in?" cried Huck. "But you let me be a pirate. You wouldn't shut me out, would you? Would you really do that?"

Tom explained that he would not *want* to shut out Huck. But he was worried about what people would say. Tom told Huck that people would say, "Hmm. Tom Sawyer's Gang! There are pretty low characters in that gang!"

Huck didn't say anything for a while. Finally, he said, "Well, I'll go back to Mrs. Douglas's house for a month. I'll try as hard as I can to stay there and be good. I'll do that, if you'll let me be in the gang, Tom."

So it was agreed. And the rest of the afternoon was spent making secret plans for Tom Sawyer's Gang.

Conclusion

This ends our story. It is just the history of a *boy*, so it must end here. If it continued, then it would be the history of a *man*.

Someday, we might look again at the people in the story. It would be interesting to find out what kind of men and women they turned out to be. But for now, it is wise not to tell anything about that part of their lives.